Dealing with DAD

how to understand your changing relationship

Other books in the
sunscreen series:

dealing with mom
how to understand your changing relationship

feeling freakish?
how to be comfortable in your own skin

just us girls
secrets to feeling good about yourself, inside and out

my parents are getting divorced
how to keep it together when your mom and dad are splitting up

sex explained
honest answers to your questions about guys & girls, your
changing body, and what really happens during sex

when life stinks
how to deal with your bad moods, blues, and depression

drugs explained
the real deal on alcohol, pot, ecstasy, and more

don't be shy
how to fit in, make friends, and have fun—even if you
weren't born outgoing

weighing in
how to understand your body, lose weight,
and live a healthier lifestyle

flying solo
how to soar above your lonely feelings,
make friends, and find the happiest you

Dealing with DAD

how to understand your changing relationship

by Joseph Périgot
illustrated by Christian Quennehen
edited by N. B. Grace

Library of Congress Cataloging-in-Publication Data:
Périgot, Joseph.
[Un père, c'est pour la vie. English]
Dealing with Dad / by Joseph Périgot ;
illustrations by Christian Quennehen ; edited by N. B. Grace.
p. cm.
Includes bibliographical references.
ISBN-13: 978-0-8109-9280-1
ISBN-10: 0-8109-9280-9 734
1. Father and child. 2. Parent and teenager.
I. Grace, N. B. II. Quennehen, Christian.
III. Title.
HQ756.P47313 2007
306.874'2—dc22
2006022785

Text copyright © 2007 Joseph Périgot with N. B. Grace
Illustrations © 2007 Christian Quennehen

Translated by Gita Daneshjoo

Book series design by Higashi Glaser Design
Production manager: Alexis Mentor

Printed and bound in China
10 9 8 7 6 5 4 3 2 1

HNA
harry n. abrams, inc.
a subsidiary of La Martinière Groupe
115 West 18th Street
New York, NY 10011
www.hnabooks.com

contents

phase 3: DIFFERENT KINDS OF DADS

phase 4: TIMES HAVE CHANGED

phase 5: WHEN DAD IS ABSENT, YOU'RE BOTH MISSING OUT

I DON'T GET MY DAD. HE'S NEVER AROUND. HE ALWAYS STICKS HIS NOSE IN MY BUSINESS. I WISH MY DAD WAS DIFFERENT. HOW AM I SUPPOSED TO DEAL?

Most people don't like to think that humans are animals. After all, we can do all kinds of things that other animals can't, like build skyscrapers, create wonderful works of art, invent new machines, and, unfortunately, go to war with each other. However, there's one thing we have in common with all other animals: Each of us has a mother and a father. Mating is essential for animals (even for snails, which have both male and female sex organs!).

If this weren't the case, nature would simply produce clones, like the famous cloned sheep named Dolly. British biologists created her from a single sheep cell. The cell wasn't Dolly's mother or father. Instead, Dolly was a copy of that original cell.

Not only would it be boring if everyone looked alike, but clones are not perfect copies of the original. If more and more copies of the original cell were made, the clones would start to look less and less like the original and nature would eventually exhaust itself.

But when a mother and a father create a baby, that baby is absolutely original and unique in the history of the entire world! Both your mother and your father were essential to making you who you are. In today's world, however, many fathers feel lost and wonder how they fit into their children's lives. Sometimes fathers even disappear. However, your father is still one half of what made you *you*. And no matter what may happen in your life, you can't change biology—your father will always be your father.

ph1

the pregnancy
partner

a baby is born . . .

. . . and so is a dad

but dad's not pregnant!

early
memories

who's your
daddy?

DAD-TO-BE

who's your
daddy?

Your cat could impregnate dozens of neighborhood cats without giving it a second thought. Several months later, he may see some kittens with the same black spot on their right paws that he has on *his* right paw, but he'll just ignore it. All animals act this way, except for some monkeys and certain kinds of birds, like blackbirds or turtle doves, which live together as couples. Why? Because it takes time, after the female becomes pregnant, for the babies to be born. The male animal simply doesn't make the connection between having sex with the female and babies being born some time later.

That's also why it took thousands of years for humans to understand the connection between men and children. In fact, it was recently discovered that a tribe of people living on a Pacific island didn't have the word for "father" in their language.

Even today, in some specific cases, the connection between a man and a child is deliberately broken. For example, women who become pregnant may choose not to tell the father and to have the baby alone. In that case, the man may never know that he's fathered a child.

It's very obvious that a woman is going to have a baby, especially in the last few months of her pregnancy. In the past, however, there was no way to tell for sure who the father was. Men would look at their children to see if they had the same eyebrows, the same walk, or the same personality. In the last twenty-five years, scientists developed genetic testing. They can compare a single hair, a drop of blood, or a drop of saliva from a man and a child and know for sure if that man fathered that child.

but dad's
not pregnant!

When a woman becomes pregnant, she realizes it very quickly: her breasts grow larger, she may become nauseated, and she may feel tired all the time or crave certain foods. Once her belly grows big and heavy, kind people offer her their seats on the bus.

Your father, on the other hand, remains standing, because the baby he's carrying isn't heavy: It's still just an idea that he carries in his mind.

This is our first pregnancy!

He knows that he created you. Even better, he wants you. Better still, he's waiting for you with an impatience tinged with fear. But his waiting doesn't have a name. His wife is pregnant, but he's not pregnant—he's only expecting a baby.

So your mother's pregnancy may not have been easy for your father. He may have felt a little distanced from the whole experience, since he wasn't carrying the baby in his body. Some men even get sick when their wives are pregnant: They get anxious or depressed, and may develop phobias and obsessions. They may even have to see a doctor.

For example, one man gained twenty pounds during his wife's pregnancy, only slightly less weight than she did! When they went to the hospital to have their baby, he ended up needing treatment as well! (He had to have a kidney stone removed.) Was that coincidence, or did some part of him want to be a part of the birth experience? We'll never know, but that kind of thing happens more often than you might think. Psychologists call this reaction "brooding" because the man tries to brood, like a hen. He wants to play the role of mother, and, since he obviously can't, he simply pretends, and his body reacts.

Dad here ... Over ...
Hey, kid, do you read me? ...

the pregnancy partner

There is a solution for men who feel left out during their wives' pregnancies: becoming a pregnancy partner. This means staying by the mother's side during every stage of her pregnancy. Perhaps your father was this type of expectant father. He never missed your mother's appointments with her doctor. He carefully kept your ultrasounds (those blurry black-and-white photographs that the doctor took of you inside your mother's womb). He read every book he could about pregnancy, even if they all said the same thing and had basically the same title: *When You're Expecting, The Baby's Coming, Pregnancy in Twenty Lessons*, etc.

He may have known as much about what was happening to your mother's body as she did!

Once a week, he went with your mother to the clinic to practice for your birth. During these practice sessions, a woman learns how to breathe in a certain way (short breaths, like a dog panting) and how to make certain physical movements in order to deal with the pain of childbirth. Your father may even have learned special breathing himself, so he could coach your mother through her labor.

As the months went on and you continued to develop inside your mother's womb, you began to be able to hear what was happening in the world outside. Slowly, you started to tell the difference between voices and sounds.

Your father loved the fact that he could already talk to you! If he put his hands on your mother's belly and spoke to you, you would swim toward his hands. This may sound like science fiction, but it's not. Psychologists have studied fetuses and how they behave in the womb and how they react to their fathers' voices. They've even discovered that newborn babies respond to their fathers' voices in the delivery room before they respond to strangers (like those doctors and nurses dressed in green scrubs—where did *they* come from?).

Believe it or not, you were able to smell your father's odor before you were born, too. The human male has a special smell. When the mother breathes in the chemical molecules that compose that smell, they pass through the amniotic fluid surrounding the baby. When you smelled your father for the first time, with your brand-new nose, his scent already seemed familiar.

a baby is born . . . and so is
a dad

Birth is traumatic for everyone. Of course, it's very painful for the mother, although she also feels intense joy and pleasure. And imagine what it's like for the baby! He's forced from a warm and cozy womb to a cold and sterile operating room. His whole world changes: He goes from liquid to air, from darkness to light. And don't forget the pain of traveling through the birth canal. It's no wonder newborns cry! Being born is a major shock to the system.

Birth is traumatic for the father as well, even if he doesn't experience the physical pain. Still, it's frightening to watch his wife endure labor and to wonder if the baby will be all right. Some fathers are so frightened by the idea of childbirth that they refuse to take part in any way. Others stand by their wives as the birth is happening, then end up fainting at the climactic moment. This is usually quite embarrassing for the father (especially since his wife had to do all the real work), but at least he has given his family something to laugh about for years to come! (If your father fainted when you were born, just accept the fact that you are destined to hear this story a thousand times during your life.)

But your father may have withstood the shock. Maybe he was calm enough to remind your mother to do her fast breathing; maybe he cut the umbilical cord; and maybe he held you in his trembling hands to give you your first bath.

Until the moment of your birth, he carried you only in his mind. Now, he carried you in his strong hands. This made up for all the times when he felt like a bystander to your mother's pregnancy. Now, he was a father.

Once the excitement of the birth had calmed down, and you and your mother were sleeping, your dad may have called friends and relatives with the good news. He may have gone home and gone to bed, only to find that he couldn't sleep. He was too busy thinking about the future of this newborn, his child, *you*.

the little mole

People used to think that a newborn was nothing more than a creature stuck to her mother's breast, needing to be fed all the time. Then we learned that a baby who has been separated from her parents for a certain amount of time at the hospital, though well-nourished, can suffer to the point of death. This strange illness is called "hospitalism." It turns out that babies can't live on milk alone. They are social animals, and have a vital need for human contact from a very early age. Babies don't see clearly before six months of age—they're like little moles—but they communicate through touch, hearing, and smell.

If you have a little brother or sister, you may have noticed that when you approach a crying baby, she quiets down almost immediately. Even before you get close enough to touch her, she can hear your footsteps. When you talk to her, she pays attention to the sound of your words. If she starts to cry again, sometimes the best thing to do is to hold her in your arms, because contact with another human being consoles her. Once she's curled up against your chest, she sniffs you with all her might, like a little animal.

Guided by these three senses, a baby grows familiar with her surroundings. First, she recognizes her mother, because she's had the most contact with her. But slowly, the baby recognizes her father, too. She even knows the difference between her father's and mother's smells and the textures of their skin.

have you been "fathered"?

When we say someone is "mothering," we mean that that person takes care of others the way a mother takes care of her child. However, "fathering" is a less-used term, even though many fathers also watch over and care for their children.

How do you define "fathering"? Well, has your father taken care of you since you were a baby? Did he take you into his arms whether you were wailing or smiling? Did he wake up in the middle of the night to comfort you when you had a bad dream? Did he care about whether you ate healthy food, got plenty of exercise, and did your homework?

Then you could certainly say that he "fathered" you, and you should

consider yourself lucky, because this kind of dad is still pretty rare (although many more younger dads fall into this category). Some dads help with their children only when they have the time, or when they feel like it. (Let's face it, taking care of kids is a lot of work!) Some men may also fear that people won't think they're "real guys" if they change diapers or give a baby a bottle. That's because boys aren't taught to be fathers.

the double
standard

Little girls are given dolls that they like to play mommy with. Parents are touched to see how their little girl cradles her doll, sings lullabies to it, and combs its hair. They enjoy imagining the day when she'll have her own children.

Even today, however, some parents would rather see their little boys

play with trucks or trading cards than with dolls. Boys who do like dolls or playing house may find that their parents discourage this. Pretty soon, they'll get the message: girls can pretend to be mommies, but boys really shouldn't pretend to be daddies.

That's one reason why many boys feel lost when they grow up and have children. They're simply not prepared—emotionally, anyway—to raise a child. Even worse, if a boy is told that it's not normal to be interested in babies, the thought may be lurking in the back of his mind that he's not a "real boy" if he is interested.

DOCTOR

early
memories

Daddy?

Recently, men have begun to realize what they're missing when they're not taking care of their babies. No one looks forward to changing a diaper, but it's fun to watch a baby wriggle, chuckle, and babble away during bath time. If you added up all the fun times, they would more than out-weigh the stinky diapers (or piercing wails in the middle of the night).

But they lose out on plenty more than these small daily pleasures. A child becomes attached to the person who takes care of him. He gets happy in that person's presence and unhappy when that person disap-pears; he calls out for him, waits for him, and beams with joy when he returns.

Humans aren't the only ones who form these strong attachments. Think about how your dog greets you when you get home from school. All that barking and jumping and running around in circles is his way of expressing how incredibly happy he is to see you.

Scientists have conducted experiments on newborn ducks that show just how strong this early bond can be. When the little ducks are shown a certain object, such as a stuffed animal, right after they're born, they never forget it. Even when they become full-grown ducks, splashing around in the pond, they get very emotional when they see the stuffed animal again.

Well, in some ways, we're all like those ducks! The relationships we develop during early childhood mark us for life. Fathers have begun to realize that they want to be a part of that first bonding. As you grow up, however, the relationship you have with your father is different from the one you have with your mother. We'll explore why in the next chapter.

affection and
authority

i ♥ mom

boy or girl?

GROWING UP WITH DAD

boy or girl?

The biggest question everyone has before a baby is born is quite simple: is the baby a boy or a girl? Should the bedding be pink or blue (or, just to play it safe, green or yellow)?

A child's sex is not a mere detail! The difference may seem small at first, but it will have greater consequences later in life—in every moment of life. And that starts in the family.

Every parent hopes, first and foremost, for a healthy baby. That matters more than the sex of the baby. However, it's normal for everyone to have their own secret dreams about what the baby will be. The way your family reacted to your sex depended on a lot of things. If your parents

already had three boys (or three girls), they may have been hoping for a baby of the opposite sex. Your mother may have wanted a boy who would resemble your father, or she may have welcomed a girl she could teach to be a woman. Your father may have hoped for a boy he could teach to be a man, or a girl he could play sports with.

Gradually, your surroundings, especially the man and the woman who raise you, help you become who you are. Believe it or not, when you're an infant you already have your sexuality! This was firmly established at the end of the nineteenth century by a famous Viennese doctor, Sigmund Freud, whose theories were scandalous at the time. Today, many of those theories are accepted. We'll discuss them in more detail next.

Oh, no ... I'm going to have another sister! Why couldn't we get a puppy instead?

i ♥ mom

In their first months of life, babies are content with their bodies and don't need anything else. Freud called this stage of life "auto-eroticism." But sexual instinct soon steers the baby toward an outside "object." This will be the person closest to him, the one who touches, caresses, and nourishes him—in most cases, the mother.

Children love their mothers. And they can feel quite jealous and exclusive about their love. (That's why you'll hear children say loudly, "She's my mommy!" In other words, not yours. So back off!) She makes the baby feel good. In return, the mother enjoys when her baby nuzzles, kisses, and caresses her. There is a loving exchange between the two.

According to Freud, if the child is a boy, a mother's tenderness has a type of sexual element. There's nothing weird about it. In fact, it's totally natural. (When little girls get a few years older, they often feel the same kind of adoration for their fathers.) Freud called the love between a mother and her son the "Oedipus complex" in reference to the myth of the Greek king Oedipus, who married his mother after killing his father. However, a child can have an "Oedipus complex" without having a life as crazy as Oedipus's. Just think of it as a symbol.

something's
missing . . .

If you're a boy, you have probably experienced the shock of discovering—perhaps by way of an unlocked door—that you and your mother aren't built the same way. She's missing something that seems pretty important to you. You may have wondered: Will she have one later in life? Or did she lose it and will get it back someday? Finally, of course, you learned the two of you will never be the same. That difference may have made you feel separate from the person you're probably closest to.

So you thought up a quick solution to keep her close to you for life: You decided that you'd marry her once you were an adult! Though your mother may have thought it was funny and couldn't help but feel flattered by this declaration of love, you quickly learned that it was impossible. After all, your mother is already married—to your father!

This is when your father stepped in. He may have found it amusing that you wanted to marry your mother, but he may also have been jealous of the mother-son relationship. He let you know in small ways that you couldn't come between the special relationship he had with your mother. For example, when you tried to slip

between them in their bed in the middle of the night, he sent you back to your own bed. It was his way of saying: "This is my space, not yours."

Naturally, you began to dislike him, this man who dared to come between you and your mother. He was your rival, and a powerful one at that. Boys often feel very competitive for Mom's attention.

In time, however, he and your mother steered you in the right direction. You learned from your father that a man can love a woman other than his mother. It's as though he said to you: "When you get older, you, too, can have a partner of your own, just like me." Once a boy accepts this, psychologists say that he's "resolved his Oedipus complex." As we grow up, we learn that we're capable of loving many people.

forgotten
memories

You probably don't remember any of these feelings from your childhood. As you read this, you may be saying to yourself, "This is ridiculous. I never felt this way. Psychologists just make all this stuff up."

That's because certain memories have been repressed, or buried or tucked away. Sometimes we bury memories if they are confusing or painful. It was painful to be cut off from your mother when you loved her more than anything in the world!

Your memory helps you deal with pain all through life by pushing negative thoughts and feelings into your unconscious, or distorting the memories so they're more tolerable. They're not exactly erased, but you can't consciously remember them.

However, even if you can't recall these memories, they actually still have an effect on you. They influence your everyday life, especially your love life, without you realizing it. They also appear in your dreams, as though they needed to come out from time to time. But they disguise themselves, which is why your dreams often seem so weird and hard to understand.

the mirror

If you're a girl, you probably never dreamed of marrying your mother. Your mother sees you, her little girl, as a mirror of herself. Of course, she has dreams about what your future may hold. She may even hope to live another life—a better life—through yours. For example, if she never made it as a dancer, she may want you to be a dancer.

But if you don't share the same dreams for your future—if, for example, you hate dancing and prefer playing with your chemistry set—then this can be a little tricky. In a healthy relationship, your mother will realize that you have to chart your own course in life and will let you quit

ballet class. In an unhealthy relationship, however, your mother may insist that you keep trying to become a dancer. In that case, she's living through you, preventing you from being yourself, which can be suffocating.

Hey, Dad, let's go to the movies, just you and me.

Once again, it's your father who can set you on the right track. He has the same kind of relationship with you that a mother has with her young son. As a little girl, you innocently flirted with your dad, and you were proud to walk in the street with him, hand in hand.

Though a boy's Oedipus complex is attached to the mother, a little girl's Oedipus complex (called an Elektra complex) can liberate her, later on, from her mother. Without the balance of your father, you might remain under your mother's spell throughout your adolescent and adult years, submissive to her desires, fearing her disapproval. Or you might feel the need to displease her. This brings us back to the same point: you're still not paying attention to what *you* want.

you're one-third
of a triangle

During the first months of your life, you understood what comfort was, thanks to your mother. You were in a bubble during the entire pregnancy, in which you and your mother's body were one.

But then you were born and, in the blink of an eye, you and your mother were no longer a couple. Now you, your mother, and your father were a threesome. This triangular life is more complicated and a lot less comfortable, but it contributes to making you who you are.

In the same way that a mother and father (or, more specifically, an egg and a sperm) were necessary for you to even exist, your parents' personalities are also necessary for you to develop your own.

Often a father is needed as a role model to teach a boy how to be a man, just as it's a mother who teaches a girl how to act like a woman. But these roles and their effects are different for everyone, and no matter what your family makeup may be, they have an effect on you.

leaving the
nest

So far we've been talking about how you interact with your parents inside the family nest. However, there's a huge world outside and, sooner or later, every child must venture out into that world on his or her own. Fathers are often your first guide to the world in which you will find your place and where you'll find a job, fall in love, make friends, and live on your own, responsible for only yourself, far from your parents.

In the nest, a father is a representative of society. It's through him that a child understands the world, with its many rules and laws. Often, he is an authority figure in ways your mother isn't. When you do something wrong, or bring home a bad report card, you may hear your mother say, "Just wait until your father comes home!" How you dread that moment! In fact, a father can exercise his authority even when he's not there. Just by thinking about her father, a child can decide to follow the rules, rather than waiting for her father or another authority figure to make her obey.

This changes to some degree during the teenage years, when children often go through an "adolescent crisis." That's when the authority that you obeyed your whole life suddenly becomes unbearable. Everything your father says or does seems wrong. You may make the wrong choices sometimes, but you have the right to do that, you say to yourself. This is a normal stage of everyone's development. A child discovers who she is by challenging her father. As irritating as it is for your father to live with a rebellious teenager, he needs to tolerate this stage in order for you to become a true individual.

Get out of the way, Ref!

affection
and
authority

Most children and teens say that they confide in their mothers rather than their fathers. Even boys, who you might expect to talk to their fathers about their problems and concerns, tend to turn to Mom instead.

There's a special intimacy between mothers and children, be they male or female, that goes back to the days when you breathed in her amniotic fluid through your little nostrils. From a physical point of view, your father was, of course, more distant. And, if his role in the family is to be the authority figure, you'll both find it hard to suddenly have him take on the role of confidant.

It's not easy to strike a balance between affection and authority, or approval and punishment. Dads often simply go with the flow—sometimes they're understanding, other times not. But there are many types of fathers, as we'll now see. You will undoubtedly find your own father among them—however imperfect he may be!

DIFFERENT KINDS OF DADS

the doting dad

the dictator dad

the distant dad

the absent dad

the buddy dad

what kind of dad?

what kind of
dad?

There's no such thing as a perfect father (or mother or child, for that matter). And every dad has his own kind of fathering style. What kind of dad do you have? Take this quiz and find out!

The Doting Dad?

The Dictator Dad?

The Buddy Dad?

The Distant Dad?

pop quiz

1. When you wake up with a fever:

A. He calls the doctor and cancels all his work appointments to stay by your side.

B. He pulls you out of bed by your feet and accuses you of faking it.

C. He winks at you knowingly, saying, "Come on, admit it! You haven't finished your math homework!" Then he writes you a sick note.

D. He leaves for work as usual. After all, his boss would never understand why he would take the day off to tend to his sick child.

2. When you bring home a bad report card:

A. He blames your teachers and says he's going to bring it up at the next parent-teacher meeting.

B. He threatens to ground you for the rest of the semester if your grades don't improve.

C. He tells you that his grades weren't great when he was in school, either, but he still managed to graduate.

D. He waits until the end of the football game on TV before reading your report card.

3. When you get home at midnight:

A. He's so glad that you're OK that he forgets to punish you.

B. He starts yelling before you've even opened your mouth to explain what happened.

C. He was asleep when you got home, but he got out of bed to hear about your night.

D. He's asleep.

creeeak

4. When he catches you flirting with someone at the mall:

A. He asks a million questions about the person you were flirting with, including (but not limited to) what grades he/she makes, where he/she lives, and what his/her parents do for a living.

B. He tells you you're not allowed to date until you're eighteen.

C. He tells you the story about his first crush.

D. Actually, he didn't even notice you were flirting.

5. When you have a party that messes up the whole house:

A. He's happy that you had a good time and helps you clean up.

B. He says nothing, because he doesn't know anything about it: you waited until he went out of town to have the party.

C. He can't say anything because he was at the party. Oh, and he's the one who spilled the soda on the carpet.

D. He lets your mom yell at you.

If your father got at least 3 A's, he's a Doting Dad. 3 B's or more, he's a dictator. 3 C's or more, he's your buddy. And 3 D's or more, he's a Distant Dad.

the doting dad

Does your father dote on you, cheer you on, constantly help you out, and (unfortunately) watch every move you make? Then he's probably a Doting Dad. Here are some more telltale signs: He inspects your homework line by line; he buys organic groceries; he only wants the best for you (which, it goes without saying, is not always what you think is best for yourself!). Though that can be annoying, it has an upside: You'll never feel that no one cares about you. In fact, you're treated like the eighth wonder of the world.

The Doting Dad is a relatively new kind of father. In the last few decades, men have started taking care of their children from day one, offering loads of care and affection. That's a good thing, right? Well, yes, unless they start clucking over you too much. A Doting Dad can be so obsessed with helping you reach your full potential that he becomes very demanding. For example, when it comes to homework, he insists that you do it as soon as you come home from school—no slacking off, ever. The same goes for TV: one hour a night, and that's it. As for filling up on ice cream or junk food? Forget it!

But deep down, you know that if you play your cards right, you can have your way with him. He'll do anything to help you. You are his life. It can be suffocating at times, but ultimately, it's reassuring.

the
dictator dad

This kind of father is an endangered species. If you ended up with the Dictator Dad, don't play the lottery: you don't have much luck. This man acts like he's living in the seventeenth century. At that time, a father had the right to imprison his son if he acted badly. And the father was the sole judge; a son didn't have the right to a trial. This kind of dad makes the laws and he enforces them. If you ask why you have to do something, he replies, "Because I said so." (And he doesn't think he should even have to answer the question.) Sound familiar?

This kind of father has one great advantage: You'll always know how he's going to react. So you plan accordingly: Maybe you throw a party when he's out of town, or you learn how to sneak out your bedroom window. You coax your mom into signing your bad report cards without showing them to your dad.

If you have this kind of dad, your teen years can be especially rough, but you have to remember one thing: If your father is a dictator, he probably had a tyrannical father as well. The pattern repeats itself generation after generation. But rest assured, you can always break the cycle.

the buddy dad

You've probably heard about all the changes that happened in society during the 1960s. Millions of young people challenged authority, whether that authority was the government or big corporations or university administrations or their own parents. Later, when those young people became parents, they raised their children in an anti-authoritarian manner, as though they didn't need discipline from anyone. The children were considered equal to their parents, whom they called by their first names.

The Buddy Dad is a product of this mind-set. He listens to your problems and understands you without imposing any rules. He doesn't act like someone who's in charge of your education, but like an equal member of the community called "our family." He's convinced that talking solves the vast majority of problems.

He's nice, but somewhat naive. Although most kids prefer this kind of father to the Dictator Dad, they also sometimes feel that he's weak. Even if they protest, kids sometimes want clear rules and someone who will bang their fist on the table and say, "No! And I mean it!"

the
distant dad

The Distant Dad may be physically present, but he might as well be in another country. His job keeps him very busy. Sometimes he even brings his work home with him, and you're not allowed to disturb him. When he's working, it's not for fun: he has to pay the bills, put money in your college fund, and save for the next vacation. Not only does he work very hard, but he's extremely tired when he gets home, so he often

Will you make it to my soccer game?

I thought you said we were going to a concert together?

wants to relax and maybe watch some television rather than spend time with you.

This description is obviously a caricature. A Distant Dad is one of the most common types of fathers. He has great affection for his kids, but in limited amounts. We can't say he lacks authority, but he hardly ever exerts it. It's like he's not really there, even when he is. Kids with this kind of dad often say things like, "I hardly see him," "We don't talk much," and "I don't think we really have a relationship." This kind of father suffers from being a stranger to his own children, but he's also practically a stranger to himself.

Go ask your mother, my plane leaves in one hour ... Love you!

the absent dad

Whether he's a Doting Dad, a Dictator Dad, a Buddy Dad, or a Distant Dad, or a mix of them all (which would come close to being an ideal father), at least your father is still around.

Many of you aren't lucky enough to have even an imperfect father at home. You have an Absent Dad, pieces of a father that you put together weekend after weekend. Or maybe you see him infrequently or never.

This is tough for a number of reasons. First, you don't get to see your dad as much as you would like. As you've seen in this book, fathers are very important to every child's life, so not having a constant dad around is a real bummer.

Second, fathers are usually absent because of divorce or separation from mothers. Sometimes, the problems in your parent's relationship are handled in a mature way—but not always. Unfortunately, the hurt and anger that your parents feel for each other can often spill over and affect you as well.

For example, your mother (or her friends or other relatives) may tell you that your father is negligent, lazy, irresponsible, or worthless. It's thoughtless for them to say this to you, but it does happen. You don't need to argue with them—after all, why create more dissent and anger?—but you need to remember that the man who other people are putting down is your father, a part of yourself. Even if he does have flaws, he'll always be your father, and that relationship is too important for you to throw away just because other people say bad things about him.

TIMES HAVE CHANGED

thank goodness it's the twenty-first century!

divorce
your dad?

who gets
the kids?

old-school dads

the new dad?

old-school dads!

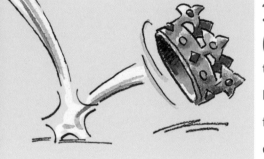

Families were very different centuries ago. Back then, the father was the undisputed leader of the family. He founded a family to continue the line of descent of his own father because the family name only continued through the male line. His mission was to ensure the security, prosperity, and growth of his descendants.

In some ways, the father acted like a king within his family. Just as the health of a country depended on a king who governed well, the health of a family depended on a father who ran things well. At some times and places in history, fathers were also thought to be in charge of their children's souls and had to watch over their spiritual development. No one doubted that the father was best for leading his family because he nourished and protected them, linking them to past and future generations.

Because his powers were so extensive, the best father to have was one who acted like a rational monarch, with a strong sense of his responsibilities and the rule of law. If that wasn't the case...well, just turn the page to find out what it would have been like to live with a dad who was really old-school!

thank goodness it's the
twenty-first century!

Imagine that a father from the seventeenth century shows up at your house and takes your father's place. If you don't behave, you might receive fifteen blows to the head. If you keep acting up, forget about getting grounded—you could be sent to prison for disobeying your father! As for your twelve-year-old sister, she doesn't need to worry about her future because her father has already promised her hand in marriage to the rich neighbor, a fifty-five-year-old widower—and there's nothing she can do about it!

This nightmare will make you wake up very grateful for your dad! Thank goodness we're living in the twenty-first century, when everything has changed. (At least in the country in which you were fortunate enough to have been born. In some parts of the world, fathers still have absolute rule over their wives and children.)

Now, children have fundamental rights. They are not their parents' property. If you are beaten, undernourished, or exploited, there are courts and law enforcement agencies that can protect you.

Hello ... Your Honor? My parents are forcing me to take Latin!

divorce
your dad?

Children have more rights today, but the threat of divorce or separation hovers over every family, no matter how close they are. Take a look at these facts:

- One out of every two marriages in the United States ends in divorce.
- About one million children are affected by divorce each year.

- About 37 percent of all children live with a divorced parent.
- By age eighteen, 25 to 35 percent of American children will be part of a step-family.

As you probably already know, either from your own experience or those of your friends, families today come in many new forms. You may live with your mother and see your father only on weekends or during vacation, or you may shuttle back and forth more frequently. Your mother or your father may have both remarried, bringing new stepsisters and stepbrothers into the mix. Or maybe one of your parents is gay and living with a new partner.

The centuries-old version of the family—a father who rules absolutely over his wife and children—no longer exists. In a way, fathers have lost their jobs as head of the family. If your father divorces your mother, he's often shut out and becomes the "occasional dad" who sees his children every other weekend. He may feel that he has little or no say in what happens to you—quite a change from the seventeenth-century dad who could send you to prison or tell you who you had to marry!

So what does all this mean for you and your dad? If your mom divorces your dad, do you have to divorce him, too?

who gets
the kids?

After the couple breaks up, the mother and father go their separate ways. They no longer live together, but they continue to look after you. Usually, a judge gives custody of the children to the mother. In some cases, a father may fight to keep his children, but it's difficult for him to get sole custody. Often, a joint custody is worked out by the courts, which means that children divide their time between their parents in a way that everyone has agreed is fair.

Anytime parents fight about who gets to see the children and when, there's a lot of anger and bitterness involved. That can be really tough for you—after all, you love both your parents. You don't want to have to choose between them!

The good news is that your parents know that you love them. The bad news is that, if you are living with your mom, your dad may be feeling very left out. He may feel unimportant, as if no one really needs him anymore. It's not your job to take care of your dad or make him feel better, but it may help you understand him a bit better if you keep this in mind.

Do you know where you came from?

Of course, I just spent the weekend at my Dad's house.

playing the
blame game

You know the saying: "Those who are absent always get the blame." In other words, when you're not around, people can talk badly about you and blame you for things you didn't do.

This may be how it is for your father, if you live alone with your mother. She is free to talk about him however she wants, since he's not there to defend himself. Because their relationship ended badly and there is tension between them, you may rarely hear good things about your father. It's important to remember that there are always two sides (if not more!) to every story.

For example, your mother may say that he abandoned you when he left. In fact, he might have left so that you and your mother could stay in

Wasn't it cool of Dad to leave you the house?

Are you trying to ruin my day?

Yes, I did my homework! Yes, I ate well! No, I didn't go to sleep too late! Any more questions?

your family home. He wanted to make sure that you wouldn't have to move to a new neighborhood, change schools, and make new friends.

Even if your mother doesn't talk badly about your father (knowing that it's unhealthy for you), she still may make little remarks that sting, such as, "Oh! Your father didn't do your homework with you! I guess he's too busy with his new life..." Such small criticisms or irritating remarks, if repeated often enough, can paint a negative portrait of your father that becomes very difficult to undo.

Your father may also be guilty of talking behind your mother's back when he sees you. Although you may not hear as many comments from him if you're living with your mother, those critical comments will also be painful. You may feel that you have to defend each parent to the other and that they're forcing you to choose sides.

If you're in this situation, see if you can talk to your parents about it. Explain to them that hearing the other parent criticized makes you feel anxious or uncomfortable, and ask them to keep that in mind. They may not stop complaining altogether (after all, it's human nature to fuss about other people a little bit!), but they will probably learn to catch themselves more often when you're around.

the new dad?

In some ways, all this turmoil can make a kid wonder whether fathers are even worth it. After all, women don't even need a specific man to have a child anymore. They can simply go to a sperm bank and get pregnant on their own (with the help of a doctor, of course!). Isn't that really a more efficient, sensible way to handle the continuation of the human species?

Of course, this is a joke. No matter how many scientific advances are made, people still want to fall in love, have children, and live together as families. In many cases, reality does not match the dream—but that doesn't keep people from trying!

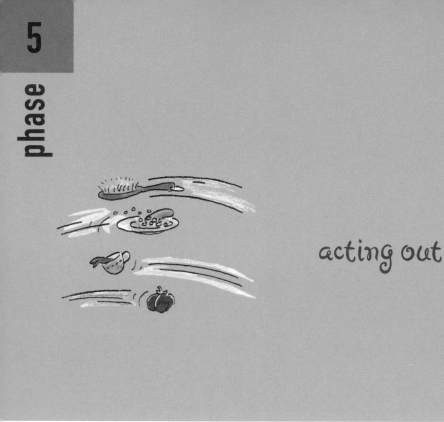

acting out

the new family

fathers of the world, unite!

thinking positively about dad

WHEN DAD IS ABSENT, YOU'RE BOTH MISSING OUT

a father without
a name

Some children face an almost unbearable situation: Their father has died or they never knew who he was. They can't talk to him or play with him. They would love the chance to argue with him or complain about him, the way their friends do about their fathers. For those of you whose fathers have died, just remember that your father is still present in the minds and in the hearts of those who loved him. You miss your father, but he accompanies you wherever you go. Even if he died when you were too young to remember him, the people in your life—in his life—still talk about him and remember him. You don't have to forget.

Other children may not know who their father is. Their mother may not

All right! I'll tell you! Your father is a math professor living in Boston.

want to name him, perhaps because she doesn't want him involved in her child's life. These cases can also be extremely difficult for the child. If you're in this situation, you may eventually want to find your father.

For example, one man searched every corner of the globe for nearly forty years to find his father. When he finally tracked his dad down, he discovered that his father was a simple man and that they had nothing in common. Nothing bound the father and son together except their biological connection. However, the son felt satisfied just knowing who his father was. When someone learns about his or her origin, there's a feeling of completeness.

A math professor...
Are you kidding?

one family,
two homes

If your parents are separated, you probably live with one of your parents in a single-parent home. Most often, it's the mother who takes care of the child. If you spend half your time at your father's home, you have two single-parent homes.

Generally speaking, you spend less time in the second home: one out of two weekends, plus half your vacation time, which amounts to approximately one-third of the year. It's good to have a primary home, a base—a place where you truly feel at home. Obviously, you can't transfer all of your belongings back and forth between two places!

There are ways to spend equal time with both your parents, but they're probably not ideal for you. One week here, one week there: sooner or later you'll find yourself without a home base, your life split in half. If your parents live far away from each other, then it would be one year here and one year there. You'd be forced to change your entire life—school, friends, etc.—and then start all over again the following year.

thinking positively
about dad

In any divorce, there's always someone who loses out, and that's you. Even if your father does everything he can to maintain close ties with you, your relationship is, to some extent, broken. There's no way you can have the constant, daily interaction that you would enjoy if you were all living together. But the lack of time spent with him isn't the worst part.

The worst is when the image you have of your father is devalued or tarnished. It's hard to live without a father, but it's even harder to live with a father if you don't respect him. Your father is your father, with all his faults, weaknesses, and limitations. He can fail you one moment of his life and succeed in another; you may even come to his aid! No one's character is ever set in stone.

That's why you should always be careful of making judgments, especially about other people. What seems like a weakness from one person's perspective might not be the case for another. You and your father need to try to understand each other—not just the good parts, but the real person. Keep talking and sharing your feelings with each other. It's the only way to really get to know a person, and one of the most important people in your life is your father.

the empty
weekend

If your parents are divorced, maybe your weekends go
something like this: Dad gets nervous every Saturday at noon, which is
when your mother is going to drop you off for the weekend with your back-
pack and a change of clothes. Maybe he is so anxious about your visit that
he even secretly hopes that something will come up and that you'll call to
say that you can't make it this weekend.

Once you get to his place, you don't take your jacket off, even when
it's time to sit down to dinner. You tell him that you always eat with your
jacket on, but he knows the truth: you're angry about the divorce, about
having to travel back and forth between your parents, and about all the
emotional distress you're going through, so you refuse to make yourself
at home.

He's carefully planned a lot of fun activities for you to do together:
going out to eat, catching a movie, visiting the zoo or a museum. . . . In
theory, he's planned all these activities to make you happy. In reality, he
wants to keep you busy. Why? Because he feels incapable when it comes
to you. Not incapable of feeding you, washing your clothes, or helping you
with your homework, but incapable of making you happy because of the
new situation.

When he drops you off at your mother's house on Sunday night, he feels both relief and shame. Seeing your sad smile as you wave good-bye makes him want to cry.

When you go inside the house, you're very quiet about what you did over the weekend. You don't like talking about it, especially not with your mother. You don't want to hear her comments about what you did with your dad. So you tell her that everything was great. But you really are thinking that the weekend seemed both too short and too long. You're feeling the same thing your father is feeling: emptiness.

the full week

Your mother, your primary guardian, has the opposite problem: The week is too full. She rushes home every evening after work so you don't have to stay home alone for too long after school. Then what seems like a whole new day begins for her: grocery shopping, cooking, cleaning, ironing; all punctuated by monitoring your homework (because your math teacher told her that you hadn't been doing very well in school since the divorce).

She's always worried about you. If she can't hear any noise coming out of your room, she checks up on you: What are you doing in there? Are you upset? She gets annoyed when you bother her about every small problem, but she can't tell you to "go ask your father."

The worst thing is that she no longer has any time for herself. You're old enough to stay home alone while she goes out to the movies with a friend. In fact, she's done that a few times, but not often—she's too tired. She spends the weekends when you're at your father's either doing nothing or catching up on sleep.

It's not easy for her to meet someone. Not only does she not have the time, she lacks the space: She hesitates to bring a new man home (and admit it, you wouldn't appreciate a new guy in the house). So she's pretty much given up on a love life, at least for the time being. She gives you all the love that she can. She lives for you and through you. Though you appreciate it, it can be suffocating. You also need to live for yourself! But at least you are certain of her love for you—that's very clear! And it's the most precious feeling of all.

who's in
charge?

Before the divorce, perhaps your father called the shots at home or perhaps he and your mother divided up the decision-making. Now that he's gone, your mother must take over, but sometimes she has neither the urge nor the ability to do so. And your new living situation—just you and her—makes things even more difficult.

We've already seen how she channels all her love to you. She's scared to death of losing you, especially if she's competing against your father. She secretly fears that, one day, you may decide that you like him more and decide to move in with him.

So she avoids forcing you to do something you don't like or punishing you. She certainly doesn't ask you to do her a favor! She tries hard not to upset you. Because you're so sure of her unconditional love for you, you take advantage of the situation, especially if you're a boy. You might decide to be rude to her until you feel guilty, at which point you act sweet again. You console her, clean up your room, and even clean up her room! You do the dishes, like a good boy or girl. Your mother then realizes how lucky she is to have you.

This scenario is classic, and you may end up acting it out over and over again. In the end, you're the one who makes the rules in the household. You're now the head of the household. But you may not really want to take on this role—after all, you're still a kid.

are you a
victim?

You might have something in common with your mother: You're both victims! Who is victimizing you? Your father. You might feel like he abandoned you both. Even if your mother asked for the divorce, she may be convinced that she had no other choice and that it's your father's fault.

But you have your doubts. The divorce happened because of your parents' problems, and you don't have all the facts. You've heard bits and pieces of their fights from listening behind the door. Nobody took the time to explain it to you in detail; instead, you were told two entirely different sides of the story.

So you probably don't really understand what your father did "wrong" and why he "abandoned" you, but every day you witness your mother suffering. You worry about her (even though you sometimes take advantage of her tough times!) and feel responsible for her. In the end, you, too, may develop a grudge against your father.

The worst is if your mother gets depressed after their separation—real depression, full of despair and anxiety that can only be treated by a doctor. That's when she seems like a real victim. Whatever she sought in the separation is quickly forgotten, swept away by her illness. Her depression is tough on you, and it's hard to not think of it all as your father's fault.

acting out

A father's absence may be even harder on a boy than on a girl. That's normal, considering a daughter learns more from her mother, even when her father is present. It can be hard for a boy to shape his identity with a mother as his only role model, especially when his father, more often than not, has been devalued. His identity as a boy is not yet affirmed. He may suffer from a lack of self-confidence.

Or maybe it's the opposite: He uses his mother as a model for how not to behave, and he builds his identity by acting in the exact opposite way of a woman—very macho! As a result, you may find it difficult to listen to your teachers. You may become aggressive or obstinate and refuse to obey the rules. If you don't take a look at how you're reacting, you may end up doing something dangerous or illegal without even knowing why you decided to do it.

Don't panic! You're not destined for a life of crime. But if you've found yourself talking back to your parents or teachers, getting in trouble at school or with the police, or taking part in dangerous activities with your friends, stop and think. Why are you acting this way? If you're trying to assert your manliness, there are better ways to do it!

Where's my soda already, Ma?

the new
family

Divorce is so painful for everyone involved that parents often think that the best solution is to remarry and make the broken home whole again. Sometimes that works, but, unfortunately, success is not guaranteed. A reconstituted family—one that includes a new parent and new sisters and brothers—can also fall apart. Then the entire process may start again with yet another new mother or father. It's a vicious cycle, especially for the children, who don't know whom to love.

A reconstituted family is stronger when a child is born into it, but that can also be more chaotic, because it creates half brothers and half sisters. Plus, the new child's biological parents both live at home, whereas the others have only one parent around all the time.

This is even more complicated than the triangular relationship that you had with your mother and father. Now, it's a pentagon, or five-sided figure, with your mother (who may also be a stepmother to your new step-siblings), your stepfather, your step-siblings, possibly a half brother or half sister ... and, of course, you.

Hi, Dave! You're my fifth daddy— and you're my favorite!

two half fathers don't make
a whole

Here's a story from a stepfather sharing his side: "My stepdaughter was four years old when I moved in with her mother. I accepted her immediately. After all, she was the daughter of the woman I loved! I knew her father, and we respected each other. He was smart enough not to accuse me of 'stealing his wife' or to blame her for falling out of love with him. But he was so troubled by the divorce that he

decided to move hundreds of miles away, which seriously limited the number of times his daughter could visit him.

"Her mother and I had a son, her half brother. But she didn't see him as a 'half'; he was, quite simply, her brother. Her real father lived so far away that she was prepared to adopt me as her own father but, out of respect for her father, I refused to replace him fully. I didn't want to add to the unhappiness and pain he would have experienced in losing his daughter—which was what I felt after losing my first two children in a divorce.

If you're only my half father, am I only half grounded?

"I was her 'everyday' father: I fed her, protected her, punished her if the situation called for it, and loved her. In my mind, however, I failed as her stepfather because I could never be her real father. I couldn't emotionally commit all the way. I merely played the role. Basically, I was her half father. The other half lived far away. But two half fathers don't make a whole."

being a
real dad

𝓕𝓲𝓯𝓽𝔂 𝔂𝓮𝓪𝓻𝓼 𝓪𝓰𝓸, when a person divorced and remarried (once, not twice!), the first marriage would be annulled, or treated as though it never existed. It was hidden away and considered almost shameful. Once the marriage was annulled, one would start all over again. The new husband accepted the children of his new wife without hesitation, and they called him "Dad."

The same scenario occurs today when the father doesn't exist, or disappears. The stepfather may decide to be a "whole" father, and not just a half father. He may not be related to his wife's children by blood, but a true father is someone who has an affectionate and educational presence in the child's life.

If you're lucky enough to have a stepfather who takes this approach to parenting, you should be willing to meet him halfway, if not more than halfway. Accept that he has good intentions toward you, welcome his care and protection, and treat him like a valued and loved member of your family.

You have every right to know who your biological father is and where you come from. But if your biological father doesn't want to—or can't—assume his role as a dad, it's OK to adopt the person who wants to adopt you. A man who is not related biologically to a child can still transform himself into a true father.

fathers of the world,
unite!

With all kinds of makeshift families in this world, can't a second father be added to the mix? In fact, it could be good to have more than one male role model as you grow up. Maybe one dad could be the one you go to when you need a soccer coach and the other could be the one you go to when you have a problem with a teacher at school. But most important, if you have two dads who both love you and want to take an active role in your life—don't shut one of them out. And don't feel torn because you should only love your "real" dad. You and your biological father have a special bond that lasts forever. Hopefully, if you have two dads, they won't try to compete with each other, but instead share in the experience of watching you grow up an experience they are both lucky to have.

fathers of the
future

Today, young men are choosing to pitch in with raising children, taking part more fully in family life, and learning more about what it means to be a good parent. Just because you might have a Dictator Dad doesn't mean (if you're a boy) that you're going to *be* one.

Remember, no father is perfect; we are all human and can't always be everything that others want us to be, but if you can keep communicating and trying to understand each other, your relationship can get stronger, or at least you can have more realistic expectations of each other. The relationship between father and child is one of life's most important experiences and, believe it or not, it's forming the kind of person you are becoming. So stay positive as your relationship with your father changes and you learn how to deal with Dad.

suggestions for further reading

Books

Girltalk: All the Stuff Your Sister Never Told You

By Carol Weston

(Harper Paperbacks, 2004)

Mom's House, Dad's House for Kids:

Feeling at Home in One Home or Two

By Isolina Ricci, Ph.D.

(Fireside, 2006)

Web sites

www.alloy.com

www.dadsanddaughters.org/index.html

www.fathers.com

www.kidsturn.org

index

about the authors

Joseph Périgot has been a philosophy teacher, a journalist, and a publisher and is now a scriptwriter and novelist. He has written a number of celebrated books for children.

N. B. Grace is a novelist and playwright who has edited numerous books for young readers. She divides her time between Austin, Texas, and New York City.